Dear Gifted Leaders,

This workbook was designed to help you navigate your function in gifted leadership. The exercises inside this workbook will help you to make some critical decisions, have meaningful conversations and hopefully make a positive impact on your leadership style. This book was created to be used in conjunction with "The Gifted Leader" Book, but it is constructed in such a way that one could use it alone. You will find many opportunities to document your success, failures and goals for the future. I urge you to use this workbook not only as a manual for gifted leadership but as a journal to help you document your progress. I would like to share with you in very certain terms; in order for this process to work, you MUST be brutally honest with yourself and those around you. I am excited for where you are, but even more excited for where you will venture in the future. Now go and be gifted!

Sincerely,

Frank James.

<u>Exercise 1 - My Gift</u>

Subject: Identifying my leadership gift!

Goal: By the end of this exercise, leaders should be able to identify what their gifts are, what other people say their gifts are and understand how their gifts are received.

1. I identify my leadership gift(s) as: Select as many as applies or fill in your own.

-Insight   _____

-Foresight   _____

-Introspection   _____

-Assertion   _____

-Active listening   _____

-Safety   _____

-Delegator   _____

-Director   _____

-Organizer   _____

-Vision Caster   _____

2. People tell me my leadership style is like:

_____
_____
_____
_____
_____
_____
_____
_____
_____
_____

3. How does what they said impact how I see me:

_____
_____
_____
_____
_____
_____
_____
_____
_____
_____

Exercise 1 Explained:

In Order to be impactful, you must understand how you deliver and how you show up. Sometimes this can be difficult to hear but honesty enhances and promotes you to operate in your gift. Oftentimes we are good at identifying things in others, but we struggle with identifying things in ourselves, especially our feelings. Be open, be honest and accept the feedback so you can become better! Use the note pages below to cite some of your learning's from this experience.

This exercise taught me:

_____

_____

_____

_____

My goal to myself and my team regarding my gift is:

_____

_____

_____

_____

_____

Notes:

_____
_____
_____
_____
_____
_____
_____
_____
_____
_____
_____
_____
_____
_____
_____
_____
_____
_____
_____
_____
_____
_____
_____
_____
_____
_____
_____
_____
_____

Notes

Gifted Leadership Tip - A leader's behavior is important! You are always being interviewed by your team. In order for them to give their all and do their best, they must believe in both you and your gift! Be careful how you show up, your success is counting on it!

-Frank James

Create Your Own Gifted Leadership Tip: Use what you have learned in this exercise and create a Gifted Leadership Tip that you can share with the next brigade of leaders. Make it a gifted one!

_____

_____

_____

_____

_____

_____

_____

_____

_____

Exercise 2 - My Style

Subject: Identifying my leadership style

Goal: By the end of this exercise, leaders should be able to identify their individual style of leadership and communicate traits that people should know about working with them.

1. I define my leadership style as:

_____

_____

_____

_____

2. Some of the things that people should know about working with me are:

_____

_____

_____

_____

3. When I show up to a project/meeting/encounter, my intent is usually to:

_____

_____

_____

_____

4. Sometimes my intent is received as:

_____

_____

_____

_____

_____

_____

_____

Exercise 2 Explained:

In order to operate as a gifted leader, it is important to be extremely honest with yourself and those you lead. If you really want people to receive from you, then be genuine about who you are and how you are received. Once people realize that you have a level of introspection and are aware of potential roadblocks in communication, they tend to be more open to the idea of being vulnerable and open in the process of teamwork and growth.

This exercise taught me:

_____

_____

_____

_____

_____

My goal to myself and my team regarding my leadership style is:

_____

_____

_____

_____

_____

_____

_____

Gifted Leadership Tip – Always be honest about who you are and how you show up. A gifted leader makes accountability (both giving and receiving) a priority in how the operate. Accountability is only uncomfortable when there is someone who lacks accepting responsibility. Do not be the unwilling participant, that will diminish your gift.

-Frank James

Create Your Own Gifted Leadership Tip: Use what you have learned in this exercise and create a Gifted Leadership Tip that you can share with the next brigade of leaders. Make it a gifted one!

_____
_____
_____
_____
_____
_____
_____
_____
_____

Notes:

Notes:

Exercise 3 - My Triggers

Subject: Identifying my triggers

Goal: By the end of this exercise, leaders should be able to communicate what their triggers are and identify who they believe are gifted leaders and why.

1. The types of characteristics that I do not work well with are: Select or fill in your own.

-Needy   _____

-Prideful   _____

-Assuming   _____

-Divisive   _____

-Drama filled   -   _____

Insubordinate   _____

-Lazy   _____

-Followers   _____

-Bandwagoners   _____

2. The types of characteristic that I do work well with are:

_____   _____

_____   _____

_____   _____

3. When I am the leader and I become triggered, I usually:

_____

_____

_____

_____

_____

_____

_____

4. In those moments, I need:

_____

_____

_____

_____

_____

_____

_____

5. My example of a gifted leader is _____ because:

_____

_____

_____

_____

Exercise 3 Explained:

In order to operate as a gifted leader, you must be able to identify the things that trigger you. You are human and it is totally acceptable to have triggers. Knowing how to deal with them is how you truly function in a gifted way. People should also know what you need from them when you are experiencing a situation that has triggered you. In general, people want to show up and perform well. The truth is, there are good days and bad days, knowing how to navigate them both really helps you to exercise your gift.

This exercise taught me:

_____

_____

_____

_____

_____

My goal to myself and my team regarding triggers is:

_____

_____

_____

_____

_____

Gifted Leadership Tips – News flash, you are human! That is the most important thing to remember always. When you are experiencing a feeling or emotion it is completely OK. Have that emotion, express that feeling but be the leader that understands how to honor the emotion but control it.

-Frank James

Create Your Own Gifted Leadership Tip: Use what you have learned in this exercise and create a Gifted Leadership Tip that you can share with the next brigade of leaders. Make it a gifted one!

_____

_____

_____

_____

_____

_____

_____

_____

_____

Notes:

Exercise 4 - My TAM (Task Attack Method)

Subject: The Task Attack Method

Goal: By the end of this exercise, leaders should be able to identify what their task attack method is and get their team to understand their style of executing tasks.

1. When I am presented with a task, my task attack method is: Select or fill in your own.

    A. Always follow the same routine.

    B. Sometimes I follow the same routine.

    C. Never remember what my last routine was.

    D. Wing it, and always get good results.

    E. _____

2. I have heard that my task attack method is: Select or fill in your own.

Brutal and anxiety provoking   _____

Smooth and executable   _____

Not ideal but attainable   _____

Exciting and invigorating   _____

3. Some things that you should know about my TAM are: Select or fill in your own.

   A. I always have multiple plans.

   B. I do not respond well to my plans being questioned.

   C. I believe that all plans should be flexible.

   D. I only share the part of the plan that is pertinent to you.

   E. I want you to be incredibly involved in developing the plan.

   F. _____

<u>Exercise 4 Explained:</u>

In order to operate as a gifted leader, you must be able to communicate to people how you work and why you work the way that you do. You must be honest about you. We all have our ways of doing things but your ability to communicate your method is what sets you apart as a gifted leader. When completing tasks, I believe that there is not always a correct and incorrect way to complete it. Instead, I believe there are just some methods that work better than others. Finding those methods and applying them to your TAM will be a game changing force in driving your success.

This exercise taught me:

_____

_____

_____

_____

_____

My goal to myself and my team regarding my TAM is:

_____

_____

_____

_____

_____

Gifted Leadership Tip – It is not the ability to make a decision that depicts a good leader. Your ability to involve people in the decision-making process is what sets you apart as a gifted leader.

-Frank James

Create Your Own Gifted Leadership Tip: Use what you have learned in this exercise and create a Gifted Leadership Tip that you can share with the next brigade of leaders. Make it a gifted tip!

_____
_____
_____
_____
_____
_____
_____
_____
_____

Notes:

Notes:

_____

_____

_____

_____

_____

_____

_____

_____

_____

_____

_____

_____

_____

_____

_____

_____

_____

_____

_____

_____

_____

_____

_____

_____

_____

_____

_____

Exercise 5 - The Perfection Complex

Subject: The Perfection Complex

Goal: By the end of this exercise, leaders will be able to identify what the perfection complex is and create solutions to not fall prey to this difficult theory.

1. When presented with a task or project, my thought process is:

   A. I just want to do what is required of me and get it turned in as swiftly as possible.

   B. When I submit something, If I get feedback to make edits, I feel defeated and then lack enthusiasm moving forward to complete the task.

   C. I just want it to be excellent and I will do whatever it takes to get it to that place.

   D. I usually do not submit it until the last possible minute as I want to ensure that it is perfect.

   E. _____

2. I chose this answer because:

_____
_____
_____

3. As a leader, I feel most validated when:

_____

_____

_____

_____

_____

One of these 4 theories are usually what happens in the mind of a gifted leader when presented with a project. Here are some things to keep in mind about each of them, respectively.

a. Most times people believe that the leaders who just want to do what is required, are underachievers or that they lack motivation. I believe that it is incredibly important to understand your strengths and weaknesses. Projects can be completely anxiety provoking and some leaders will overthink and over complicate something in order to appear as if they are deeply engaged in a project. The reality is, in gifted leadership things are continually changing. It is completely appropriate to submit a project when it is completed if you are happy with the product you are presenting.

b. Gifted leaders are passionate! Sometimes feedback can feel like more of a weapon than an asset. When a leader responds with defeat, that usually is indicative of some trauma that the leader has experienced in a past project or situation. While it is important to recognize and deal with that trauma, you must be self-aware and introspective enough to realize when that is leading your plight. Feedback to a leader is essential and can really edify your skills and capabilities if you allow it to enhance your gift.

c. Excellence is key and using the "by any means necessary" approach can really help gifted leaders go the distance. More often than not, the first draft is usually not the final draft. In fact, the first draft normally serves as the ground level support to build the finished product on. Like in any structure, the foundation is key in order to have an excellent final product. If the foundation is shaky, there is no way possible to have a good landing spot. All your gifts and tools used together to present something that is well thought, comprehensive and concise should always be your goal. Be gifted and be excellent!

d. Waiting to the last possible minute to submit something in fear of it not being perfect is a direct example of the perfection complex. The perfection complex creates an illusion that the end goal is final and exact. It limits the possibility of growth and expansion. As a gifted leader, you must be flexible and open to the idea that things can and will change often. Change is appropriate for getting to the best possible place of completion. Evolution is inevitable so do not allow perfection to stifle your growth.

e. _____
_____
_____
_____

This exercise taught me:

_____

_____

_____

_____

_____

_____

My goal to myself and my team regarding my perfection complex is:

_____

_____

_____

_____

_____

Gifted Leadership Tip – Stop allowing past mistakes to negatively impact how you move. Yes, you should learn and grow from your shortcomings as they are inevitable, but that feeling you get when you have fallen short, do not use that to fuel the perfection complex. It only complicates things more!

-Frank James

Create Your Own Gifted Leadership Tip: Use what you have learned in this exercise and create a Gifted Leadership Tip that you can share with the next brigade of leaders. Make it a gifted tip!

_____

_____

_____

_____

_____

_____

_____

_____

_____

Notes:

_____
_____
_____
_____
_____
_____
_____
_____
_____
_____
_____
_____
_____
_____
_____
_____
_____
_____
_____
_____
_____
_____
_____
_____
_____
_____

Notes:

_____
_____
_____
_____
_____
_____
_____
_____
_____
_____
_____
_____
_____
_____
_____
_____
_____
_____
_____
_____
_____
_____
_____
_____
_____
_____
_____
_____
_____

Exercise 6: The ICE Method

Subject: Cultivating Gifts

Goal: By the end of this exercise, leaders should be able to help other leaders develop their gifts by using the Impartation, Communication and Execution method of Gifted Leadership.

1. The leader of this exercise should pass out the ICE plan exercise sheets and have participants complete them. (See Next page).

2. After all papers have been collected, the leader should have general discussion around how people felt about completing this exercise.

3. The feedback I received was:

_____

_____

_____

_____

_____

_____

_____

4. After hearing the feedback, the leader should work one on one with each person to develop their ICE plan in order to help get them to their next level in leadership.

Exercise 6 - ICE Plan Handout:

1. The goal that I would like to achieve/having trouble achieving is:

_____

_____

_____

_____

_____

_____

2. In order to achieve this, I feel like I need:

_____

_____

_____

_____

_____

3. The best way for me to receive feedback and assistance is:

_____

_____

_____

_____

_____

_____

Exercise 6 Explained:

In order to be a leader that cultivates other leaders, it is critical that you understand completely what their goals are. Sometimes, leaders tend to give people goals instead of asking them what they want. People rarely rebut or disagree with their leaders when they feel like they have commissioned a plan for something they believe they would be great at. While you should always speak life into your leaders, it is important to include them in the process. Sometimes, you need their insight to mix with your foresight in order to get them where they ultimately want to be. Surely this may come with some bumps along the way and some areas where you must detour, but do not allow your desire to get in the way of their journey.

This exercise taught me:

_____
_____
_____
_____

My goal to myself and my team regarding the ICE method is:

_____
_____
_____
_____
_____

Gifted Leadership Tip – No one wants to work in an uncomfortable environment. When you as the leader are on a quest to help other leaders and you make decisions for them, that works as a detriment to their process. In order to appreciate the destination, one must be involved in the journey. -Frank James

Create Your Own Gifted Leadership Tip: Use what you have learned in this exercise and create a Gifted Leadership Tip that you can share with the next brigade of leaders. Make it a gifted tip!

_____

_____

_____

_____

_____

_____

_____

_____

_____

Notes:

Notes:

Exercise 7 - Tough Conversations:

Subject: Having Hard Conversations

Goal: By the end of the exercise, leaders should be able to understand the nature of tough conversations and what it takes to navigate them.

1. Identify what you believe tough conversations are: (Select as many as applies or fill in your own)

-Termination   _____

-Failed Projects   _____

-Suspensions   _____

-Feelings/Emotions   _____

-Loyalty   _____

-Culture Changes   _____

-Roles   _____

2. Of the conversations identified above, please write down the 3 that you are most uncomfortable with dealing with or speaking about.

A. _____

B. _____

C. _____

3. These types of conversations are uncomfortable for me because:

_____

_____

_____

_____

_____

_____

Exercise 7 Explained:

When you are a leader, vulnerability must be something that you are ok with working through. In leadership they way that you are received is largely predicated on your level of vulnerability. In my research, I have found that most of the time people buy into the leader before they buy into the message that you are trying to give. This is especially important when having to navigate tough conversations. They are a part of the leadership process and people need to understand that this comes with the territory. If you have presented yourself in such a way that you are faultless, it is less likely that people want to receive corrections from you. Always be honest and be clear. Never leave people wondering what their actual issue was or what the reason for the tough conversation was in the first place. A gifted leader should be clear and kind.   Always remember the Triple R method when participating in tough conversations.

Remain - Remain present in the conversation. Present does not necessarily mean calm, but it means you are actively engaged in what is happening now.

Remind - Remind them of how we made it to this moment. Sometimes we can get so involved in only the present issue that we fail to make mention of the journey that led us to this landing spot.

Reassure - Always reassure them that this conversation is not one sided. You want to know, hear and see things from their perspective so that ultimately the best decision is made. You will find that sometimes, it is simply a failure in the communication style that landed you in this tough conversation.

This exercise taught me:

_____

_____

_____

_____

_____

_____

My goal to myself and my team regarding tough conversations is:

_____

_____

_____

_____

_____

_____

Gifted Leadership Tip – It is impossible to navigate leadership without participating in tough conversations. They are inevitable and required. Do not run from these conversations as you gain a lot of knowledge from them. The leader who passes at the chance to engage in tough conversation, lacks the capacity to become a gifted leader.

-Frank James

Create Your Own Gifted Leadership Tip: Use what you have learned in this exercise and create a Gifted Leadership Tip that you can share with the next brigade of leaders. Make it a gifted tip!

_____

_____

_____

_____

_____

_____

_____

_____

_____

Exercise 8 - Interview Me

Subject: Identifying my leadership culture

Goal: By the end of this exercise, leaders should be vulnerable enough to express to their team what type of leadership culture they function in.

1. The type of working culture that I operate in is:

   A. I run a tight ship and do not like many questions.

   B. I like an environment that is open and structurally unstructured.

   C. Extremely fast paced, organized and goal oriented.

   D. Slow and steady but thorough and comprehensive.

   E. _____

2. The positive feedback that I have heard regarding my leadership culture is:

   _____
   _____
   _____
   _____
   _____
   _____

3. The challenging feedback that I have heard regarding my leadership culture is:

_____

_____

_____

_____

_____

_____

4. The changes that I want to make regarding my leadership culture are:

_____

_____

_____

_____

_____

_____

<u>Exercise 8 Explained:</u>

One of the most valuable things that a leader can do is express and communicate their culture to the team. This takes vulnerability, intentionality and transparency. People usually select jobs on much more than the wage and location. People oftentimes heavily consider the leadership culture and environment. It is critical that you are honest with yourself and transparent with your team about who you are and how you operate. Some leaders are open and welcome to changing and enhancing while others are not. You are constantly being interviewed by your team. Knowing this, consider the thought that if you got an employee to come, how much are you willing to do to get them to stay!

a. In this type of leadership culture, it is important to manage expectations upfront. Some people enjoy a self-driven environment where they can go and flourish without the need to continue and ask questions. Not everyone wants to offer input, challenge the status quo or offer insight on a project. Some people just want to be. While this is true, it is important that people know this when they begin. This type of environment can cause a great employee to begin to feel unappreciated and unwelcomed thus sending them, your team and your culture in a complete whirlwind.

b. Open environments can be great. The one thing to remember when you have this type of culture, there must be some rules to engagement. While it is awesome to consider ideas and make changes along the way, you must be careful that you are not building frustrations due to a lack of committing to the task and following it through. The AR^2 method (Analyze, Resolve, and Reset) is especially important in this kind of culture. People need to know how and when to submit as well as start over and regroup.

c. Fast paced environments are common. While this is true, it is important to understand that fast paced does not mean unstructured. There are many things that require a great deal of attention but also a truly short timeline of completion. It is important to understand who your movers and shakers are so that you do not overwhelm the entire team with this kind of environment.

d. There are some people who never "look busy" yet they get the task complete. In this type of culture, the check-ins are critical. Sometimes, people get into a motion and can execute large amounts of production while other times it is just slow and steady. When you see this, do not necessarily assume there is a problem. Use your check-in to see where your people are and engage them from there. Thoroughness and comprehensiveness are two things that should never be compromised when working towards a project or goal. They should be the epitome of what you do!

e. _____
_____
_____
_____

This exercise taught me:

_____

_____

_____

_____

_____

_____

My goal to myself and my team regarding my leadership culture is:

_____

_____

_____

_____

_____

_____

Gifted Leadership Tip – Leadership requires connection, connection requires relationship. Without relationship it is impossible to be a leader.
-Frank James

Create Your Own Gifted Leadership Tip: Use what you have learned in this exercise and create a Gifted Leadership Tip that you can share with the next brigade of leaders. Make it a gifted tip!

_____

_____

_____

_____

_____

_____

_____

_____

_____

Exercise 9 – Making Decisions

Subject: Identifying my decision-making process

Goal: By the end of the exercise, leaders should be able to describe their decision-making process and offer insight into their thought process.

1. When I am required to make decisions, I consider the following:

   _____
   _____
   _____
   _____
   _____

2. When I am required to make decisions, I DO NOT consider the following:

   _____
   _____
   _____
   _____
   _____

3. The feedback that I receive from my team on my decision-making process is: Select one.

   a. Loosely considered in making my next decision.

   b. Is great information to know but I will generally continue with my method.

   c. Completely transforms the decisions that I make moving forward.

   A. A leader that only loosely considers the thoughts and opinions of direct feedback from their team can cause chaos. The last thing that you want on a team is chaos. People tend to lash out when they feel like their voice is either unheard or unappreciated. As the leader you must make the best decision, however that decision should be made with feedback from the people who it directly effects.

   B. A leader that is dismissive will lose people quickly. People want to see and be seen. To disregard someone because you believe that your process is the best way and the only way, speaks of immaturity in leadership. It is critical to work towards the common goal of making the whole better. If we are not doing that then we are merely just wasting time.

C. This is a gifted response. When you can receive information, dissect it and then make changes on how you move forward, that is the type of leader who has developed a great culture within their establishment. There will be some things that are unable to change due to protocols but working towards a solution to consider making someone or something better is a great environment to operate in.

Exercise 9 Explained:

As a gifted leader, it is detrimental to your success that you understand your team is your GPS. They are speaking and leading; do not miss your exit because you are stuck on your own path. You are the leader and that cannot be taken from you, but you must allow input from your team in order to make the best decisions possible. People usually buy into the leader before they could ever buy into the vision. If this is done out of sequence, you will find yourself stranded on an island alone.

This exercise taught me:

_____

_____

_____

_____

_____

_____

My goal to myself and my team regarding my decision-making process is:

_____

_____

_____

_____

_____

_____

Notes:

Notes:

www.ingramcontent.com/pod-product-compliance
Lightning Source LLC
Chambersburg PA
CBHW060008050426
42448CB00028B/2469